Holy Cross Catechetics Office
MW01678924

You're Dreaming!

learn about Religion

Kevin O'Donnell

Hodder & Stoughton
LONDON SYDNEY AUCKLAND

Acknowledgements

The publishers would like to thank the following for their permission to reproduce material in this volume:

Unwin Hymen, of HarperCollins Publishers Ltd for the extracts from *The Lord of the Rings* and *The Silmarillion* by J R Tolkien.

Every effort has been taken to trace and acknowledge ownership of copyright. The publishers will be glad to make suitable arrangements with any copyright holders it has not been possible to contact.

The Publishers would like to thank the following for their permision to reproduce the following copyright photographs in this volume:

Ancient Art and Architecture Collection 18r; Andes Press Agency 33r, 35l; Roger Bradley 35r; Bridgeman Art Library and Keble College Oxford 17r; Dennis Coutts 24; P Emmett 25l, 26; Robert Harding Picture Library 34r; K Johnston 12, 33t; NASA 40, 44; Anne and Bury Peerless 30, Picturepoint Ltd 18l, 24; Mel Thompson 28, 32, 33b, 34b; Topham Picture Source 9, 14, 15, 16, 20, 21, 23; ZEFA Picture Library 17r, 31, 36, Cover.

Cataloguing in Publication Data is available from the British Library.

First published 1993

© Kevin O'Donnell

0 340 57147 0

All rights reserved. No part of this publication may be reproduced or transmitted in any form or by any means, electronically or mechanically, including photocopying, recording or any information storage and retrieval system, without permission in writing from the publisher or under license from the Copyright Licensing Agency Ltd. Further details of such licenses (for reprographic reproduction) may be obtained from the Copyright Licensing Agency, of 90 Tottenham Court Road, London W1P 9HE.

Printed for the educational publishing division of Hodder & Stoughton Ltd, Mill Road, Dunton Green, Sevenoaks, Kent by Colorcraft Ltd., Hong Kong.

Contents

Start Here!

Symbols can be very powerful. They move us and make us feel things. Many symbols are used in the world's religions.

In this book, we will be studying fire, water, light, darkness, food, trees, symbolic stories and dreams.

For the Teacher

Two Stories

I used to be stone deaf. I would see people stand up and go through all kinds of gyrations. They called it dancing. It looked absurd to me until one day I heard the music!

A story was told about a temple that had a thousand bells. This sank, one day, into the sea. The legend said that the bells still pealed out, and could be heard by anyone who would listen. A young man heard of this, and he would sit for days by the sea trying to hear the bells. Finally he decided to give up the attempt. Perhaps he was not destined to hear the bells. Perhaps the legend was not true. It was his final day, and he went to the shore to say goodbye to the sea and the sky and the wind and the coconut trees. He lay on the sand and, for the first time, listened to the sound of the sea. Soon, he was so lost in the sound that he was barely conscious of himself, so deep was the silence that the sound produced. In the depths of that silence, he heard it! The tinkle of a tiny bell followed by another, and another, and another... and soon every one of the thousand temple bells was pealing out in harmony, and his heart was rapt in joyous ecstacy!

The Rationale of this Book

This book follows on from *I Wonder*... as an introduction to basic religious concepts and feelings. It is concerned with symbols in life and religion, a key concept with which pupils should be familiar before they launch into studies of religions. An understanding of the symbolic is an important tool for a deeper study of religion and much may be lost and dismissed without this. It is all too easy to teach facts about religions without laying the proper foundations, and not being sensitive to pupil's presuppositions and background.

This book follows the spirituality approach, recognising the necessity of teaching the existential dimension of religion as well as the other dimensions.[2] A true phenomenological approach will include this, and not be limited to an objective, factual study. Too much work on symbols stops at this point - 'here is a Buddhist Wheel of Life, a Christian Cross, a lighted candle, or the Sikh holy book'. Religion is fuelled by spirituality, commitment, devotion, feelings, fears, hopes and experiences. Something of the drama and power of the symbolic needs to be experienced, however fleetingly, by those studying the subject. Symbols are powerful and mysterious; they probe deep feelings; they have an ambiguity, perhaps coming more alive for some than for others, and suggesting a glimpse of the transcendent that eludes our rational grasp.

Through the study of symbols, we hope to help the pupils to 'listen to the temple bells' of creation and to look deep within themselves. We seek to break open the materialistic presuppositions and introduce the spiritual dimension. Our society suffers from a good deal of religious repression, in the sense that *religious* experience has been marginalised by the overwhelmingly *intellectual* nature of our educational system.[3] In a fast-paced, media-sensitive and highly visual society it is difficult simply to sit down and listen, and to be in tune with the deep things within themselves. Metropolitan Anthony tells the down- to-earth story of a woman he taught. She had prayed but never felt the presence of God. He simply told her to sit alone in her room, relax in a comfortable chair, and to knit! In the quietness, she felt a presence in the silence. She simply had to sit still.[4]

Symbols and their Meaning

A symbol is far more than a sign or object that stands for something else. Symbols evoke the meaning, the truth, or the presence of what they represent. Paul Tillich spoke of a symbol's participation in the reality it symbolised - a flag was intimately bound up with the nation-state it represented, and passions of loyalty and pride. Jung argued that symbols expressed eternal truths, and saw them as possessing a numinous power akin to a spell. They surface in dreams and still exert their power on a largely secular society. Symbols are coded psychic charges that channel spiritual power.

While many symbols have a universal character, a local element should also be noted, as has been stressed by recent anthropological studies.[5] A particular gesture in one society might mean something completely different in another. The value of these symbols lies in their role in social bonding rather than in their conveying of universal meanings. Wittgenstein has reminded us in this century that it is the *body* which is foundational in the origin of human discourse, rather than some phantom, disembodied private language of the soul. We communicate through social interaction; our gestures and activities form concepts and terms. He saw the emotional as being just as powerful as the rational in this process, and criticised Frazer's rationalisations of the material in *The Golden Bough*. Ritual drama and religious expression are a vital part of human communication. We are worshipping, awe-stricken, passionate beings.

Theology and Symbols

Symbols are central to theological discourse because we are dealing with the transcendent. Buddhists refer to symbols as 'rafts' to help them in their journey. In the great religions, symbols are like fingers pointing to God, and thus have a provisional, limited nature.

When Thomas Aquinas stopped writing, someone asked him why. He replied; 'Some months ago I experienced something of the Absolute, so all I have ever written about God seems to me now to be like straw.'

A study of symbols helps with an awareness of the limitations of language, with its stretched, elastic nature as we try to catch hints of the Beyond.

Religious narratives are richly symbolic; sometimes this can produce debate and discussion. The story of the temple curtain tearing when Jesus died is probably meant to be symbolic, but the stories of his virgin birth and resurrecion, while containing symbolic details, are hotly defended as historical events by most Christians. A religious tradition's sensitivities to its stories and symbols should be understood and respected, rather than attempting to impose a personal interpretation upon them.

Meditation and Fantasy

The use of meditation techniques and guided fantasy helps to open up the existential dimension of the topic being studied. These engage the feelings and perceptions of the pupil directly. The meditation techniques are based upon neutral relaxation exercises and do not use the approach of TM or any particular religion. This type of exercise for deeping awareness of faith has been used in Christianity, (eg *The Spiritual Exercises* of St Ignatius Loyola) whereby one enters into the Gospel stories imaginatively and in some forms of Buddhist practice where pictures of various people are seen in the mind to encourage disinterested love.

A Final Story

The Zen Master Ryokan lived a very simple life in a little hut at the foot of the mountain. One night, when the master was away, a thief broke into the hut only to discover that there was nothing to steal.

Ryokan returned and caught the burglar. 'You have put yourself to much trouble to visit me,' he said.'You must not go away empty handed. Please take my clothes and blanket as a gift.'

The thief, quite bewildered, took the clothes and slunk off.

Ryokan sat down naked and watched the moon. 'Poor fellow', he thought to himself, 'I wish I could give him the gorgeous moonlight.'[6]

That is our task, to open eyes to see the moonlight!

Notes

1 From Anthony de Mello *The Song of the Bird*, Doubleday, New York, 1984

2 See Ninian Smart , *The Religious Experience of Mankind* Collins, 1971 for an exposition of the six dimensions.

3 See Solomon Asch's discovery of the group pressure which can affect decision making, using an experiment with pieces of string of different lengths. When most people in the group urged that they were the same length, others complied against the evidence in front of them (David Hay, *Exploring Inner Space*, Penguin, London 1982, p205.

4 Metropolitan Anthony, *School for Prayer*, DLT, London 1970.

5 As for example, in the work of Durkheim, Levi Strauss, and more recently in that of Victor Turner and Jonathan Smith. Turner stresses that symbols work together to create *communitas*.

6 *ibid.*, de Mello

Meditations and Guided Fantasies for use with chapters in this book:

Chapter 2 A meditation on dream symbols (see p14).

- Sit still and breath deeply and regularly.
- Count ten breaths.
- Imagine that you are tired, and your body feels like lead. You are sinking down into the chair.
- Then a gentle breeze blows over you, and into you. Take a deep breath in. Imagine it filling you like a balloon.
- Imagine that you start to rise up and fly like an eagle, above the classroom and out over the town. Soar through the clouds. What do you see? How does it feel?
- Return to your seat, slowly, count ten breaths.

Chapter 5 A guided fantasy related to Moses and the Burning bush (see p27)

- Still yourself.
- Imagine that you are walking in the darkness and you see a fire on the horizon.
- You walk towards this and you see a bush on fire with intense heat, but it has not burned up.
- You look into the middle of the fire, and see white light. This bathes you, and you tingle all over.
- You fall down on your knees, head bowed, perspiring.
- You feel the white light bathing you,and washing all around you. It feels good and warm.
- Imagine being bathed in this light for a few minutes. Feel its power, its holiness and its love.
- Count ten breaths and then open your eyes. Paint a picture of the fire that you saw.

Chapter 5 A guided fantasy related to The Easter Fire (see p25)

- Still yourself
- Imagine that you are lying down on the floor. Your body is tired and heavy. You can hardly move. It is a great effort to lift a finger.
- A bright fire surges over you and you feel its warmth. You are feeling numb and tingling inside.
- Suddenly, you feel a rush of energy flowing into you. You leap up, and jump up and down, laughing and dancing.
- Count ten breaths and then open your eyes.

Chapter 6 A guided fantasy on Calm Down! (see p31)

- Close your eyes and breath slowly.
- Imagine that you are lying beside a river or pool.
- Listen to the different noises around you, in your imagination.
- Feel the cool breeze blowing over you.
- Keep imagining the scene, breathing slowly. Open your eyes and end when ready

Chapter 7 A guided fantasy related to Holy Communion (see p35)

- Sometimes things go wrong, but we find a new start and happiness again.
- Still yourself by sitting quietly and breathing sets of ten breaths.
- Imagine that you are in a dark room - it could be anywhere so long as it is a strange place to you. See what pops into your mind.
- You try to switch on a light, or light a match, but for some reason you can't. Perhaps you can't find the light switch, or the matches are all used up. You feel frightened, and you start to perspire.
- Look around the room, feel your way around. Is anything familiar?
- Suddenly, a glow comes through an opening under a door, or through the curtains. You look out and you can see the sun starting to rise. It gets brighter and brighter, until you are flooded with golden light. It feels good, and warm and safe.
- You can see the way out, and you run outside, feeling free and happy.
- Count ten breaths and then open your eyes.

Chapter 8 A meditation on The Cross (see p38)

- Still yourself by sitting and breathing.
- Imagine that you have a very heavy load on your back. You are walking up a hill. Feel the straps cutting into you, the sweat pouring down your face. Your shoulders hurt as you take each step. You push yourself up the last stretch on your hands and knees.
- When you reach the top, the straps snap and the pack rolls off your back and tumbles down the hill. Stand up and stretch, breath in the cool air and feel how free and light you are. Run around the mountain top.
- Count ten breaths, then open your eyes.

Chapter 8 A guided fantasy on The Trees of Valinor (see p39).

- Still yourself
- Imagine that you are on mound of earth and you hear beautiful music.
- You see two shoots sprouting up as the music continues.
- One tree grows tall. You see dark green leaves opening up that shine as silver on one side.
- The other grows tall, and you see bright green leaves that have golden edges. Light and colours sine from them.
- You stand and watch them, feeling their warmth on your face and hands. Some birds and animals dart to and fro around them. What animals do you see?
- They start to dim, and then one bursts out in silver light again.
- Count ten breaths and then open your eyes.

Ask the class to use their fantasy imagining to draw or paint a picture of the Two Trees of Valinor.

Chapter 10 A guided fantasy on The Return of Christ (see p45)

- Sit comfortably and breathe deeply.
- Imagine that everything is dark. You are walking down a staircase. There are cobwebs, and you feel chains around your legs and arms. Others are stumblimg down with you.
- Suddenly, a bright, white light appears and lights up the stairs. You feel it burning on your face. You feel warm all over, and you tingle from head to foot.
- There is a beautiful figure looking at you. It points a sword and cuts all the chains.
- You run up the stairs, free!
- Count ten breaths and then open your eyes.

Chapter 10 A guided fantasy on Ragnorak (see p46)

- Still yourself and breath softly.
- Imagine that you are running from the battle of the gods. You run and run, through a thick forest. You hide in a huge tree that has been hollowed out.
- You hear crashes, and thunder, and screams.
- You see flashes of light and fire.
- You fall asleep in the dark, damp tree. Everything is dark.
- You wake up, and feel soft sunlight on your face. You get up and walk into the open air. Stretch. Yawn. Breath the new, clean air. Reach up and take a leaf, filled with dew. Drink the dew. It tastes cool, fresh and sweet. Splash the dew over your head, and look at the sun rising over the green valley.
- Take in the view. Count ten breaths, and then open your eyes.

1 Symbols

Special signs on a map help people to find where they are going to. The sign is not the real object itself; it only stands for it. There are many signs like these, such as roadsigns.

What do you think this stands for?

Some symbols stand for ideas and feelings, and not just objects.

The love heart suggests that two people are joined together in love. Perhaps they are unable to think of anything else, and if they are away from each other, it will feel painful. They have been stricken by love's arrow.

The dove suggests peace because it is white, suggesting goodness, and because it is gentle. The dove was the bird sent out after Noah's flood to see if the rains had stopped. It brought back a piece of an olive branch as a sign that the waters were draining away.

A flag suggests not only a country, but also all the feelings of pride and loyalty its people might have in it.

THINGS TO DO

1. Think what symbols you see around you in a typical day. Draw these and say what they stand for.
2. Design a new symbol for peace.
3. Design a badge or a flag for yourself that symbolises something about yourself, or something that you really like.

You'll Never Walk Alone!

Many of the people who took part would not have described themselves as religious. Yet they felt they had to do something like this. One person said 'It was a way of lifting the burden off them. Y'know... the grief'. Another said that it was something he had to do; 'It was something that came from within'.

The Hillsborough disaster in Sheffield shocked people in Liverpool. Many fans had been killed in the crush against the barriers during a football game at a ground in Sheffield in April 1989. Though memorial services were held in the Roman Catholic and the Anglican Cathedrals, many people felt that something more had to be done to express their grief.

One person came up with an idea. He had seen a blue teddy bear sitting on an altar in one of the services, with two scarves wrapped round it, one red and white, one blue and white, the colours of the two Merseyside teams Liverpool and Everton. Before long, a committee had been formed to collect scarves from across the city. The plan was to tie enough scarves together to link Everton's ground with Liverpool's ground. Transit vans, nicknamed 'scarfmobiles', were sent out to collect the scarves, Exactly one week after the tragedy, at 3.06pm, the final scarf was linked. The pitch at Anfield, Liverpool's ground, was strewn with bunches of flowers.

People sang, and wept, and waved the opposing teams' scarves in the air.

The remarkable thing was that many people gave their most precious mementos, things that it must have taken a lifetime to collect. They brought them to the football ground as an offering, a little sacrifice, to show their grief.

THINGS TO DO

1. Imagine that you were present at the Anfield service. What does it feel like to be there? Ask someone next to you why he or she has linked up the scarves.
2. Some people gave their most precious mementos. What things are precious to you?
3. Sometimes people need special actions and symbols to say how they feel.Can you think of some more everyday examples - such as on birthdays?
4. Why do you think people offer you a drink when you visit them? What are they really saying to you?

Set the Prisoners Free!

This is the symbol for Amnesty International, a group that works to set certain kinds of prisoners free. In some countries, people are arrested and sent to jail just for having ideas that are against the government. Perhaps their only crime is belonging to a group that speaks out against the government. These people are called *prisoners of conscience*.

Amnesty campaigns to set them free, regardless of their religion or politics, as long as they have not been involved in acts of violence. Volunteers write thousands of letters to the leaders of the country, as well as to the prisoner, hoping to pressure people into releasing him or her.

The candle suggests hope, and the barbed wire suggests the prison. If people know they are remembered, then they have hope.

Sometimes children are imprisoned because they are related to people who speak out against the government, or just because they are innocent bystanders who get in the way. One such incident happened in the Philippines to Feliciano Morales when he was ten years old. Some soldiers were fighting near his home and his two elder brothers were shot. Feliciano and his father ran, but they were caught. Feliciano was put into prison.

THINGS TO DO

1. Draw the Amnesty symbol and explain what it stands for.

3 Write to Young Amnesty at 99 -119 Rosebury Avenue, London EC1R 4RE for details about young prisoners. Perhaps you could do something as a class to help them.

Words! Words! Words!

Some things are *facts*, such as 2+2=4, or that water boils at 100 degrees centigrade.

Some things are expressions of how we feel. We have many words that work like this -

We also use poetry to really say how we feel about deep things in life. So, a person in love can say 'My love is like a red, red rose...'

We also speak through movements of our bodies. A raised hand can be a warning to stop, friends shake hands (originally to show they had no weapon concealed) and we clench our fists when we are angry.

We can draw things that stretch our ability to understand. Look at the drawing below and see if you can work it out!

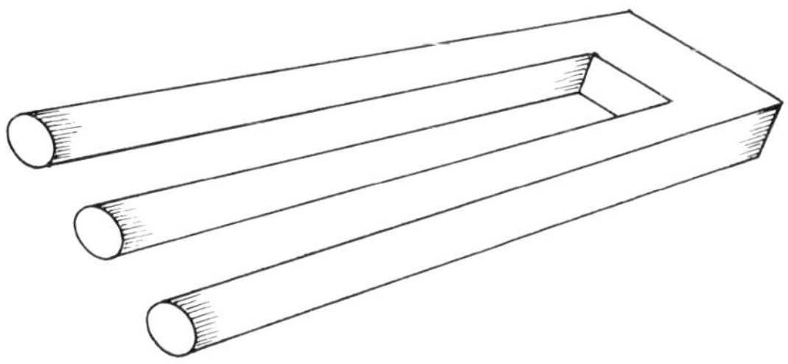

Life is sometimes like that; it is a mystery that we cannot put into words. Where did we all come from? What are we apart from chemicals and atoms? What happens when we die?

Look at this symbol. What do you see? Some people will see a Nazi swastika. This image will send shudders down the spines of people who lived through the Second World War. It will suggest a great evil. However, others will see a symbol for good luck, or for life! The swastika is much older than the Nazi use of it.

The swastika is similar to an ancient symbol that is still used by Hindus today to symbolise good fortune. The image points in all directions; it suggests wholeness and God's Blessings

Some symbols, then, can mean one thing to one person, and something completely different to another!

THINGS TO DO

1 Try to write a sentence to describe how:

- an orange tastes
- what it feels like to be peeling a strong onion
- what a flower smells like in the spring
- what it feels like to think about life after death.

2 Divide into pairs. Each pair thinks up a short story or situation. You both have to mime this, i.e. speak only with your bodies! Act out your story in front of the class, and see if your mime is good enough for people to follow what is going on.

3 Draw a swastika on a large piece of paper and cut out the shape. Then, one one side, say what you think many people would feel when they see this. On the other side, say what it would mean to a Hindu. Can you think of any other symbols that might mean different things to different people?

2 You're Dreaming

What happens when we dream? Here are some ideas:

Sifting through the Day
Our brains do not completely switch off when we are asleep, and so we dream about things that we have been doing.

Sometimes dreams can be very mixed up, and sometimes they tell a story, in a sequence. You might wake up wondering how your dream was going to end.

Deep Feelings
We might dream symbolic dreams, where different things that happen to us stand for something. We might be frightened of something, and this appears in our dream in a disguised, or exaggerated form. Running from a monster might be a story your mind makes up because you are frightened of facing up to something.

Messages from God
People in ancient times believed that all dreams came from God, or the gods. They had wise men and priests who used their own special techniques for interpreting them. Many people believe that this was superstitious, though some believe that God might still give people a dream *sometimes*, but this would be an extra special dream with a clear and powerful message.

Dreaming the Future?
Some people claim to have had dreams about things that happen later on. So, for example, a person will dream about a plane crash, and on the news the next day hear about such a disaster.

It is hard to prove that this was more than a coincidence, but the world we live in is a strange and wonderful place!

THINGS TO DO

1 Make a dream cube out of a sheet of card or paper. Before sticking it together, write about the different ideas of why we dream on four of the sides. On the remaining two sides, draw a picture of a scene from some recent dreams that you can remember.

2 Have you ever woken up wanting to know how your dream would have ended? Describe your dream and your feelings on waking up.

3 What is the most striking dream you can remember?

4 Have you ever thought that you have dreamed the future? Do you believe you can predict the future by dreaming?

Joseph's Story

The Hebrew youth, Joseph, had been sold into slavery in Egypt, and his master's wife had him thrown into prison for something he did not do. While there, he was asked to interpret the dreams of two other prisoners. One was the chief cupbearer to the Pharaoh, and the other was a baker.

The cupbearer dreamed of a vine with three branches, with clusters of grapes. He filled his cup with wine from these and took it to the Pharaoh.

The baker dreamed that he was carrying three trays of cakes, and the birds ate the ones on top.

Joseph told them the interpretations. The cupbearer was going to be released in three days and given his job back serving the Pharaoh. The baker, however, was to be taken away in three days and hanged, when the birds would peck at his body. (You can read the story in the Bible, Genesis 40).

Joseph was summoned to interpret two of the Pharaoh's dreams.

First of all he saw seven fat cows coming from the river Nile, followed by seven thin ones. The thin cows ate the fat ones!

Then he saw a stalk with seven ripe ears of corn, followed by one with scanty ears of corn. The ripe ears were swallowed up by the scanty ones.

Joseph explained that the dreams both spoke of seven years of plenty, followed by seven years of famine. The Pharaoh then ordered that food should be collected during the years of plenty and stored for the famine years. (You can read about this in the Bible, Genesis 41.)

THINGS TO DO

1 Explain what the different things in the dreams of the cupbearer and the baker stood for.

2 Imagine that you are the cupbearer and then the baker writing your diary after Joseph has told you the meaning of your dream. Explain what has happened, and how you feel about it.

3 Have you had any striking dreams that have stood for something important in your life?

Dream Symbols

How does this photo make you feel? Make a list of your feelings.

Flying
Many people dream, at some point, about being able to fly. Comic books are full of characters like Superman who can fly. Flying can suggest freedom, soaring above everything in the fresh air. Flying can suggest escape from trouble. A common dream is of being cornered by attackers, and then discovering that you can fly away.

Being Chased
We often dream about being chased, perhaps by soldiers, or gangsters, or a UFO! We might be worried about something, and this is how the worry shows up in our dreams. Someone might be angry with us, or might be scaring us. Sometimes we might just dream about being chased with no obvious reason why. Maybe our brain is just telling stories in our sleep.

Falling
We sometimes dream about falling. We might be jumping out of an aeroplane, or in a car falling off a cliff. Falling suggests feeling insecure and worried. Something is not quite right. But notice how we always wake up before we hit the ground!

Meeting a Mysterious Stranger
Sometimes we dream that we meet someone in our dreams whom we do not know. It can be a man or a woman, an alien, or an angel. We might enjoy an adventure with this person, or they might tell us something we need to know. These strangers are really parts of ourselves. There are bits of ourselves that we are not always aware of. These stories in dreams are symbols of our deep feelings.

THINGS TO DO

1 Divide into four groups and talk, respectively, about dreams you have had about flying, being chased, falling, or meeting a mysterious stranger. Take the most striking dream from each group, and draw a comic strip of this, working as a group. Ask your teacher to display these around the classroom.

2 Design a poster about flight, and write a poem to say how you think it would feel to fly.

4\. Read Isaiah 40:28-31 in the Bible. How is flight used as a symbol here?

Going Underground

Another common dream is about going down into a dark and hidden place. Many people are fascinated by caves and places under the ground. Some find them frightening, too!

Theseus and the Minotaur is an ancient story (or myth) about a journey underground.

The king of Athens once killed the son of the king of Crete in battle. In revenge, the king of Crete conquered Athens and sent seven young men and seven young women to Crete each year. They were forced, one by one, into the labyrinth, a series of passages under the palace. There they were devoured by a monster with a man's body and a bull's head, called the Minotaur. One year later, the son of the king of Athens, Theseus, offered to go to Crete. Ariadne, the daughter of the king of Crete, fell in love with him and secretly gave him some thread and a sword.

Theseus laid a trail with the thread, and he faced the Minotaur and killed it. He followed the thread back to the surface and returned to Athens in triumph.

There is a factual basis to this old story. There was a large palace at Knossos in Crete which was discovered by Sir Arthur Evans in 1894. Evans found a complicated drainage system beneath the palace, which might well be the origin of the labyrinth in the story. There are also altars with bulls horns around the palace that suggest that a bull god was worshipped there.

Whatever the facts, this myth was a powerful and popular story told by the ancient Greeks. It remains powerful, for it tells us something about ourselves. We often bury things that we do not like deep within our minds. We try to forget them. Sometimes these hidden fears and thoughts pop up in dreams as monsters or people we are afraid of. Going down into darkness suggests going down into the depths of our own minds to find things that we have tried to forget. By facing up to some of these things, we can overcome our fears. Theseus faced the Minotaur, and came out to freedom!

Going down underground can also make people feel warm and secure. It reminds them, deep down, of being in their mother's womb, safe, warm, and looked after.

THINGS TO DO

1. We have all got a Minotaur inside us! What things are there that you don't like about yourself? What are you most afraid of? Think about this for a few minutes, privately.
2. We have all got a Theseus inside us, too! Think of all the things you like about yourself.
3. Think of a time when you really have felt safe and warm. Write a few lines about this and draw a picture showing the details of this time.

3 Light

Light is an important symbol, suggesting various things:

Light gives life!

There would be no life on earth if we did not have sunlight. Plants could not grow, and then there would be no oxygen for us to breathe.

Try an experiment sometime. Take two young plants. Place one in a dark place, and one in sunlight. See which one grows faster.

Light suggests hope

We talk about 'seeing the light at the end of the tunnel'. People walking in caves or down potholes will look for sunlight to find their way out. Light suggests hope, when everything around us seems hopeless.

Light shows us the way

Light helps us walk through darkness, to find our way, and to help us find the right path. Sometimes, in cartoons, when people have good ideas, they are shown with a lightbulb above their heads. We talk about having 'seen the light', or about being 'enlightened' when we work out an answer to a question, or the correct way of doing something.

Light symbolises life, hope and truth (finding the way). The Amnesty International candle, shown in chapter one, is a way of symbolising hope - light burning in the darkness. In many political uprisings (such as those in Eastern Europe in 1990) people lit candles to symbolise their hope and their quest for a better way of life.

THINGS TO DO

1 Write a short story, imagining that you wake up one morning and you find that you have gone blind. Just as suddenly, at the end of the day, you regain your sight. Write about how you feel, and how you cope.

2 Tell a story to the class about a time when you were lost, and how you found your way back to your home.

3. Working in pairs, each think of a time when you suddenly saw the answer to a problem - when 'the penny dropped', or you 'saw the light'.

God as Light

The Muslim holy book, the Qur'an, has a passage where God is compared to light;

> Allah is the light of the heavens and the earth. His light may be compared to a niche that enshrines a lamp, the lamp within a crystal of starlike brilliance. It is lit from a blessed olive tree neither eastern nor western. Its very oil would almost shine forth, though no fire touched it. Light upon light; Allah guides to His light whom He will...
>
> His light is found in temples which Allah has sanctioned to be built for the remembrance of his name. In them morning and evening His praise is sung by men whom neither trade nor profit can divert from remembering Him. (Sura 24)

The Hindu holy book, the Gita, says of God;

> Could a thousand suns blaze forth together it would be, a faint reflection of the radiance of God. (Gita Chapter 11)

THINGS TO DO

1 Think of all the things that light symbolises. Why do you think that God is compared to light?

2 Paint a picture called 'The Light of a Thousand Suns'. Perhaps you could work in groups.

Christians too compare God to light.

> God is light, and in him there is no darkness at all. (1John1:5)

They believe that God lived as one of us, as Jesus, who said:

> I am the light of the world. Whoever follows me will have the light of life and will never walk in darkness. (John 8:12).

This picture, by Holman Hunt, is called The Light of the World. *Jesus carries a lamp to show the way to go. He knocks on a door, symbolising people's lives.*

There are a number of stories about Jesus healing blind people. These stories were told not only to demonstrate the power people believed that Jesus had, but also to stand for his power to make people see spiritually. The healing of a blind person was a symbol of his power to make people turn from their sins and to see the way to God.

THINGS TO DO

1 Design a collage that shows how people are spiritually blind; show warfare and other hurtful things, and place a picture of a light (a sun, star, candle) in the middle of them.

Festivals of Light - Chanukkah

Chanukkah is a Jewish festival of light. This takes place around December (25th of Kislev in the Jewish calendar). A special, eight-branched candlestick, called a *menorah*, is used during the festival. (Sometimes there is a smaller, ninth candle from which the others are lit.) One candle is lit each day until all eight are burning on the last day. Party games are played on`the Sabbath.

This festival is held to remember a battle won by the Jews over 2,000 years ago. Their country was controlled by a foreign king, Antiochus, who did not believe in the Jewish faith, and who tried to stop people following it. A statue to a foreign god was placed in the Jewish Temple, which offended the Jews.

Judas Maccabeus (a nickname, meaning 'The Hammerer') led a group of Jewish freedom fighters who drove the invaders out of their country. Judas entered the Temple and looked for some oil to light the seven-branched menorah that always used to burn in the Temple to remind people of God's presence. He could only find a small pot, holding enough oil enough for one day only. It would take eight days to make some more! Yet, miraculously, this oil actually lasted for exactly eight days. Many saw this as a sign of God's favour.

The picture below show an occasion when the Jews were cruelly treated. It depicts Roman soldiers carrying away treasure from the Temple in Jerusalem after they destroyed it in 70 CE (you can see the menorah) There have been many harsh times for the Jewish people, and the Festival at Channukah reminds them of this, and of God's promise to stay with them.

THINGS TO DO

1. Draw a Chanukkah menorah at the top of a page, and then write eight sentences about the Festival; include what happens and what it is based upon.
2 What do you think the menorah lights symbolise?
3 Can you think of a time in your life when things were hard, and then they then got better? Write a few lines about this, then say if there was anything which helped you cope at the time (for example, perhaps you were very ill, and people came to see you and bought you nice presents).
4 Imagine that you were a young Jewish person at the time the Romans were carrying all the treasures out of the Temple. Write a letter to a friend saying how you felt.

Festivals of Light - Divali

Divali is a Hindu festival of light. (The word 'Divali' means 'row of lights'.) This festival usually takes place in October or November, and lasts for three to five days. The festival ends on Divali day, followed by New Years' Day. Houses are cleaned for days before the festival, and on Divali day, lights are placed in windows. Brightly coloured patterns are drawn on the floors of houses. All debts are settled, and account books are closed. Family quarrels are sorted out in readiness for the new year. The goddess Lakshmi is worshipped to bring good fortune and wealth.

An old story is retold at Divali about Prince Rama fighting the evil demon King Ravana. Ravana has ten heads, and siezes Rama's wife, Sita. After a chase to Sri Lanka, Rama kills Ravana with his bow.

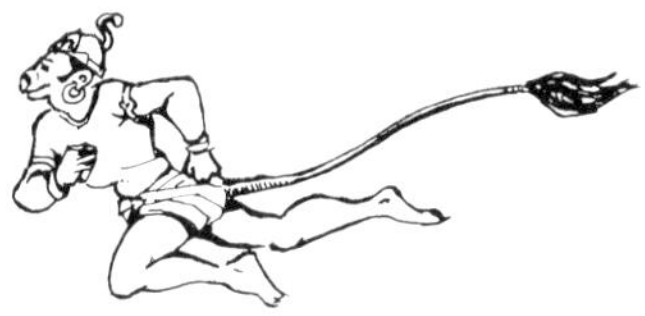

Hindu children act out this story, and paper images of Ravana are burnt at the end of the festival. The story symbolises the struggle between good and evil going on inside each one of us. At the New Year, Hindus think about this as they hope for peace and prosperity in the year to come.

THINGS TO DO

1 Why do you think lights are used at Divali? What do they symbolise?

2 Working in pairs, talk about New Year's resolutions that you have made and broken!

3 Think of a time when you have been angry with someone and you have sorted out the trouble. Write a few lines about this.

4 Darkness

Darkness suggests fear and evil to many people.

Fear

We are often afraid of what we cannot see, or of what we cannot understand. Children are sometimes afraid of 'things that go bump in the night', or squeaky floorboards, or patches of light reflected on the wall from gaps in the curtains. Who hasn't pulled up the bedclothes to hide at some time in his or her childhood?

People grow out of this fear, but walking about in the house in the dark is always strange. Nothing seems the same. The fear of the dark probably goes back to ancient times, when our ancestors were afraid of wild animals that would attack them at night.

If you still are sacred of the dark, try telling yourself that you are still in your room. Tell yourself that the large shadow is your wardrobe. Think of its shape and what you keep inside it. Reach out and touch the nearest thing to you, perhaps an alarm clock. Feel its shape. Tell yourself what it is. Then sing a song to yourself. You might want to say a prayer, too.

Evil

By evil, we mean things that are not just spooky and strange, but things that hurt people - wars and famines, football riots and earthquakes flattening cities.

Mystery

Darkness can also symbolise mystery. We often say that we are 'in the dark' about something when we do not know about it.

Life is full of mysteries. It is like a detective novel with the last page missing, so we cannot easily find out all the answers. Think of these:

- What happens after we die?
- Is there a God?
- Are there such things as ghosts?
- Are there UFOs?

What other things can you think of?

THINGS TO DO

1. Write a few lines about a time when you were scared of the dark. What happened? What were you actually frightened of?
2 What helped you to stop being scared of the dark?
3 Can you think of something that you think is really evil? See if you can find a cutting from a newspaper or a magazine
4 Produce a short project on one of life's mysteries, with illustrations.

Letting go!

We have to learn to let go of many things as we go through life. We might move house, and have to get to know a new town, and make new friends.

Some young people feel deeply about the move from primary to secondary school. Suddenly, they are in a new place that seems huge. They used to be the older boys and girls, now they feel very small and young!

We also have to let go of some things that we love. When a pet dies, it is painful and sad. Something has been lost. But we cannot really love anything unless we are also able to give it up.

"Some horrible things happen, like famine, diseases, disasters or wars. There can't be any meaning in life! We all happen by accident, and life is one big struggle for survival."

"No, I disagree. Life is full of good things like, love, friendship, music and beautiful things in nature. There must be meaning in it all!"

Many people ask the question, "If there is a God, then why is there so much suffering in the world?" It is a difficult question to answer. People suggest different answers.

It's our fault!

We can choose between right and wrong. We are people, not robots! We choose to fight wars, to build bombs, to torture and to pollute the earth. Some famines are made worse by our stupidity and selfishness (not treating the soil right; wars stopping relief supplies getting through).

Just testing!

Some think that pain and suffering are like a test, making us fight hard for what we believe in. Some say their pain can make them closer to God. (Others have been hurt so badly they find this hard to believe. 'God is love, not a tyrant', they say.)

Under construction

Others say that the world is not finished yet. It is not yet as it should be. It is like a huge work of art that God is still working on. So, a struggle is going on between good and evil.

Believers say it is more important to try to change the world than to explain why there is evil in it.

A Kurdish refugee stumbles while carrying his sick wife to a rescue helicopter: Turkey 1991.

THINGS TO DO

1 Make a list of all the changes that you felt when you moved to secondary or middle school. Talk about these in class. (If you have not yet made that move, try to imagine what it will be like.)

2 Think about things that you have had to let go of. Talk about this in pairs. Then write about them, saying how you felt at the time.

3 Look at the photo above. Then look at the two quotes in the first column. Does the photo illustrates these? Give reasons for your answer.

4 Draw a picture strip to show how some people explain why God allows evil .

5 Why do you think many people want a religious service to remember their dead after a disaster? Do you think people turn to God in a crisis?

The Shadow!

J.M. Barrie's story *Peter Pan* is about the adventures of a boy who has no shadow. Peter Pan lives in NeverNever land, where people do not grow older. Eventually, he finds his shadow, and he is then able to grow up

Shadows are dark things, and they are often used to symbolise evil. Of course, we all have a physical shadow too! There is a side of us that we do not really like. We have all done things we do not like and have hurt others. We might not wish to admit this, even to ourselves.

Part of growing up or becoming wise is to face up to the wrong things in our lives and our actions. We need to admit there are parts of us that are not very nice, and then we need to try to do something about them, but we have to accept who we are, every little bit of us.

There are good, creative things in us, and things we are not so proud of. There is anger, and pride, and selfishness. Some people open up to the dark side, their shadow self, much more. They feed it and get worse

We may feed the good side more, but it is temtping to ignore the shadow self. Then we are dishonest. By denying a part of ourself, we do not work properly. This is why religions urge people to confess what they have done wrong, to face up to it, and to make a fresh start. Here is a confession prayer from the Anglican Church in New Zealand

> We need your healing, merciful God: give us true repentance. Some sins are plain to us; some escape us; some we cannot face. Forgive us; set us free to hear your word to us; set us free to serve you.

The priest then says:

> God forgives you; forgive others; forgive yourself.

THINGS TO DO

1 Talk or write about a time when you did something hurtful. Did you say 'Sorry' or did you keep on feeling guilty?

Evil Powers

Sometimes so much evil is unleashed in the world, such as the killing of many Jews and other people who spoke out against Hitler in the Second World War, that some people believe that there must be an evil force or spirit at work, stirring people up to turn to evil.

Starving and exhausted people in Belsen concentration camp.

Evil is very strong and powerful, and some people can be overcome by it. We do not really understand what it is. In the past, different races had a god of evil, such as the trickster god, Loki, in the Norse (Viking) myths. One Viking writer described Loki in this way:

> **There is also counted among the heavenly powers one whom some call the Mischief Maker of the gods and the first father of lies ... Loki is handsome, easy on the eyes, but, inside, the soul of spite and completely fickle.**

In the ancient world, people had many ideas about gods and demons, forces of good and evil. They knew, as we do today, that evil was a very powerful force. Some believe that there is an intelligent, evil force, as well as the wrong things in our lives. Some believe that there is a personal devil.

The Devil

In the Jewish, Christian, and Muslim faiths, there is the devil, or Satan, and his demons. These spirits try to thwart God's work in the world, and they influence people to do evil. But the devil is never described in the Bible or Qur'an as having horns, a tail and hooves; those were ideas formed in the Middle Ages.

In traditional Jewish, Christian and Muslim belief, Satan is supposed to have been an archangel who rebelled and fell from heaven, taking some rebel angels with him. He is powerful, but very much God's inferior. He should not be understood as God's shadow self or evil side. God is holy ('God is light, and in him there is no darkness', as the New Testament puts it.) There will come a day when the devil will be destroyed forever. At the moment, there is a spiritual war going on in the world.

Many believers think there is some sort of personal devil out there; but some feel that the idea of Satan is a symbol for the evil we do to ourselves, which is all too real and powerful.

THINGS TO DO

1 Do you think there is a personal evil power? Discuss this as a class.

2 Some people think the devil is only a symbol. What do they think the devil symbolises?

3 Some people still believe in the reality of evil spirits. Have you heard any stories of people's experiences? (Not counting fantasy films and novels!) Do you think these could be explained any other way?

4 In the Christian Bible, read Revelation 12:7-12. Draw a picture of the scene described.

5 Fire!

A modern recreation of the burning of a Viking longboat

Fire suggests different things to us. Fire can be a symbol for power, purity and love.

Fire is powerful - it can burn and destroy whole buildings or forests. A small spark can set a huge fire ablaze in a dry forest and destroy thousands of trees.

Fire purifies - it destroys rubbish and kills germs. Surgical instruments can be sterilised by passing them through a flame. The great Fire of London in 1666 stopped the spread of the bubonic plague because it destroyed both the germs and the rats, the carriers of the deadly disease.

Fire suggests warmth and love - a family sitting around an open fire, or friends around a campfire. There is warmth in their hearts as well as in their bodies. When two people are in love, they feel a 'fire' inside them, full of passion.

The earliest humans were fascinated by fire. They learned the secret of making fire by rubbing sticks together to create sparks by friction. Ancient people saw fire as a gift from the gods, as a sacred thing.

The Greeks told a story about Prometheus who stole fire from the gods to give it to humans, for which the gods punished him! The Vikings laid their dead warriors in longships, surrounded by their most treasured possessions, and then set them ablaze. For them fire was a holy thing, a gift from the gods. It took away the body of the warrior.

THINGS TO DO

1 Write a story imagining that you are a fireman fighting a blaze in a building.

2 Write a few paragraphs about a warm, cosy time with family or friends. (This might have been around a campfire, at a barbecue or at home.) If you have a spare photograph of this, stick it into your books, too.

3 Why do you think ancient people thought fire was a gift from the gods?

4 Find out the story of Prometheus from a book about Greek myths in the School library and write your own summary of it.

5 Imagine that you were to be given a Viking warrior's funeral. What special objects of yours would you want people to put into the longboat with you?

The Easter Fire

Christians celebrate the resurrection of Jesus at Easter. They believe that he is alive in a new and spiritual way. Many Christians have a special ceremony to symbolise Jesus' victory over death, and his presence with them. When people go to Church on the evening of Holy Saturday, the day before Easter Sunday, they find a bonfire blazing away outside.

In the Roman Catholic service, the priest says

> 'Dear friends in Christ, on this most holy night when our Lord Jesus Christ passed from death to life, the Church invites her children throughout the world to come together in vigil and prayer....'

The fire is blessed;

> Father, we share in the light of your glory through your Son, the light of the world. Make this new fire holy, and inflame us with new hope...

The candle is then lit and carried into the church. Three times the priest says,

> 'Christ our light',

to which the people respond,

> 'Thanks be to God.'

The candle is placed on a stand at the front of the church. This candle is called the *Paschal Candle*.

A song of triumph is sung, called the *Exultet* which starts with the words:

> Rejoice heavenly powers! Sing choirs of angels!
> Exult, all creation around God's throne
> Jesus Christ, our King, is risen
> Sound the trumpet of salvation!
> Rejoice, O earth, in shining splendour,
> radiant in the brightness of your King!
> Christ has conquered! Glory fills you!
> Darkness vanishes forever!...

Christians rejoice that night because they believe that Jesus rose from the dead. He gives them a hope beyond death.

- The fire suggests ***power*** - Jesus rose again; death is defeated.
- The fire suggests ***love*** - God the Father did not leave Jesus in the world of the dead.
- The fire suggests ***holiness*** - it symbolises the mystery and the goodness of God.

THINGS TO DO

1. Draw the Paschal candle. What does it symbolise?
2. Read through the words of the *Exultet*. How do these make you feel?
3. You can read one of the accounts of the resurrection of Jesus in John 20:1-23. Read Luke 24:13-34, also. Here, the risen Jesus appeared to two disciples. How did they say they felt during this episode?

Holi

The Hindu festival of Holi is a spring festival. It falls on the full moon of the Hindu month Phalguna (sometime around February-early April). This celebrates life, joy and love and is a fun time for all the family. In India it is celebrated for three days, but only for one day by Hindus in England. Jokes and pranks are played, but these are more restrained in England than in India. (There, people throw coloured water at each other!) The festivities begin with an evening visit to the temple.

The temple is lavishly decorated and hymns of praise are sung. The highlight of the service is the passing of the *Arti* tray. This features an array of flickering oil lamps at which the people warm their hands before passing it on. Before they receive the Arti tray, though, they say this prayer;

> Lord, lead me from the wrong paths to the right,
> from all wrongs to truth,
> from darkness to light,
> from death to immortal life.

An arti tray being passed round.

Outside, a bonfire is lit and people walk and dance round it. Coconuts are offered to the fire. These are later taken out and eaten.

The fire represents warmth as well as the power of God bringing life to the earth after the cold winter months. The victory of good over evil is recalled by telling an old story about a time when the king of the demons ruled the universe. His son, Prahlad, refused to worship his father and prayed to God instead. His father tried to kill him, and had Holika sit him on her lap on top of a bonfire. (Holika could walk through fire unharmed.) However, she had forgotten that she was only safe if alone, and the fire consumed her! Prahlad escaped alive, and, eventually, the demon king was overthrown.

Coconuts are a symbol of food and of life as they contain both milk and flesh.

THINGS TO DO

1 Imagine that you are visiting a Hindu temple with a friend. You watch the Arti ceremony and enjoy the sight of the fun around the bonfire later. Ask your friend what the ceremony means. Write down your friend's answers in the form of a dialogue between the two of you.

2 Draw an Arti lamp and write the prayer 'Lord, lead me...(shown above)' in its flame. Underneath the lamp write down some things that you would like to see improved in your life, or in the world around you.

3. Draw a comic strip to tell the story of Holika and Prahlad.

4 Think of all the ways in which Holi shows that good triumphs over evil.

Moses and the Burning Bush

The Hebrew Bible tells this story of the call of Moses.

> Moses had fled from Egypt after killing an Egyptian guard who was treating the Hebrews brutally. The Hebrews were slaves at the time, used as forced labour to build new cities for the Pharaoh.
>
> Moses tended sheep in the desert, living with the tribespeople there. One day, he thought he saw a bush on fire. Fearing the damage that this might do, he ran over to look at it. As he approached it, he realised that something was wrong. It was on fire, but though it appeared to be burning up, the bush was not harmed.

> When the Lord saw that Moses was coming closer, he called to him from the middle of the bush and said, 'Moses! Moses!'
>
> Moses answered, 'Yes, here I am.'
>
> God said, 'Do not come any closer. Take off your sandals, because you are standing on holy ground. I am the God of your ancestors, the God of Abraham, Isaac, and Jacob' So Moses covered his face, because he was afraid to look at God...(Exodus 3:46)

Moses felt God was telling him to go back to Egypt to set the Hebrews free.

> 'I know all about their sufferings, and so I have come down to rescue them from the Egyptians and to bring them out of Egypt to a spacious land.'

Moses felt God promise, 'I will be with you...'

The Bible story suggests that Moses had a *vision*. Anyone else present would probably have seen only a normal bush but Moses saw something special. Some people claim to see visions at times, and they believe that this is one way that God speaks to people. Others wonder whether they are just imagining it. Whatever Moses saw, it changed him. He had the courage to go back to Egypt and to confront the Pharaoh. Eventually, he led the Hebrews to freedom.

The fire in the bush suggests God's power, his holiness, and his love. Moses felt that God was powerful enough to set the people free. Moses felt scared in front of the bush. He took off his sandals as a mark of respect at God's request.

THINGS TO DO

1 What do you think the fire says about God in the story?

2 Have you ever been in a situation where you suddenly found the courage and strength to do something that that you never thought you could?

3 Read the full story of Moses and the Burning Bush in Exodus chapter 3.

6 Water

Water, rushing, gurgling past us, or lying calm and still in a pond, water attracts us and fascinates us. Water is used as a symbol for many things. Water can suggest ***Life***, ***Death***, ***Peace***, and being ***Washed clean***

Life

Water gives us life. It refreshes us when we are hot and thirsty; it makes things grow; it turns a desert into an oasis of lush greenery and teeming wildlife.

Death

Water can be dangerous. If we are not careful, we can drown in it!

Peace

Lying down beside still water is soothing and relaxing.

Washing Clean

We feel clean all over, new and fresh after bathing or taking a shower.

THINGS TO DO

1 Write a few lines about a time when you have felt refreshed or relaxed when near water.

2 Talk as a class about times when you have been scared in water (your first swimming lesson, perhaps?)

3 Write a poem about how it feels when you step out of the bath.

Christian Baptism

Baptism among the Tswana people of Botswana

The first Christians probably baptised people in rivers by dipping them under the water. Gradually, the children of Christian parents were baptised even though they were too young to understand what was happening to them. It was thought to be wrong for children to miss out on the blessings given to their parents. But, some other Christians feel that you should wait until the children are old enough to speak for themselves.

The water of baptism stands for three things:

Death
Baptism is a sign that someone has 'died' and left his or her old way of life and started a new one, believing in Jesus.

Christians use water as a special symbol in *baptism*. Some churches baptise a person by pouring water over his or her head three times. Other churches baptise in a pool of water by lowering a person beneath the surface and quickly lifting him or her out again. Baptism is done only once in a person's life and is the sign that the person has become a Christian and joined the Church. Jesus told his followers to baptise people:

> Go, then, to all peoples everywhere and make them my disciples; baptize them in the name of the Father, the Son, and the Holy Spirit...(Matthew 28:19)

THINGS TO DO

1 Why are some people baptised?

2 Describe the two different ways that baptism can be done.

3 Why did Christians start to baptise people?

New Life
Baptism is a sign that a person is starting a new life given by God.

Washing Clean
Baptism is a sign that a person has been washed clean of their guilt for all the wrong things they have done, and that God has forgiven them.

THINGS TO DO

1 Design a poster or a collage called 'Baptism' that includes the idea of new life and being washed clean.

2 Think of a difficult and unhappy time which changed into one that was much happier. Talk about this in class.

3 Think of an occasion when you felt bad about something you had done and then you were let off. How did you feel?

Muslim Wuzu

This photo shows the Muslim practice of *wuzu*. Muslims wash in a certain way before they say their formal prayers. They wash the mouth and the nostrils, the hands up to the elbow, behind the head and the ears, and feet. They do this because they believe that God (Allah) has commanded them to do so, and that his instructions were revealed to the Prophet Muhammad, and included in the Qur'an, their holy book:

> Believers, when you rise to pray wash your faces and your hands as far as the elbow, and wipe your heads and feet to the ankle.....Allah does not wish to burden you; He seeks only to purify you so that He may perfect His favour to you, so that you may give thanks. (Sura 5:6)

The Muslim faith began in Arabia where it was sandy, and the areas to be washed in the wuzu ceremony are those that would easily become dirty feet, hands, face and head. This is a mark of respect to God. It is like getting ready to meet an important or respected person; most people would bathe and put on their best, clean clothes. In Islam a similar respect is paid to Allah.

Muslims are expected to pray certain, set prayers five times a day; these are called *salat* prayers (they can say their own, made up prayers as well).

THINGS TO DO

1 Draw a sign for a Muslim house or place of prayer giving instructions how to perform the wuzu.

2 Why did the Prophet Muhammad say that God (Allah) had ordered people to wash before prayer?

3 Why did the early Muslims, living in desert areas, wash certain parts of the body and not others?

4. Why do Muslims believe it is important to wash before praying?

5 Have you ever had to appear before someone important, or before the public? What preparations did you make? How did you feel?

6 Some other religions do not think it is necessary to wash before praying. What is your opinion? Does anyone in the class belong to a religion that has different washing ceremonies ?

Calm Down!

Still water calms and relaxes us. It is cooling, too, on a hot day, to be near water. One reason why water calms us like this may be that we used to float in liquid in our mother's womb, and somewhere, deep down, we may have a memory of this.

There was a wise and holy monk who lived alone in a cave. A young monk went to visit him to ask him to be his teacher.

You know how to pray and how to be still you are so at peace with yourself! Teach me!

'Very well', said the wise monk. 'Go and fill that bowl with water from the river.'

The young monk did so, and he placed it at his teacher's feet. 'Now, look into it and tell me what you can see' said the wise monk.

'Nothing,' replied the younger one, 'I can only see mud from the river.'

He put the bowl down, and a little while later, the wise monk called his pupil to him. 'Now, look again. What do you see?'

The young monk looked, and smiled. Now, he could see his own face.

So, that is how it is with prayer and meditation when your mind is still, you can listen to God, and to deep things in yourself!

THINGS TO DO

1 What is the moral of this story?

2 What does the cloudy water suggest about the young monk's state of mind?

3 Retell this story in a comic strip.

4 Can you think of a time when you have been worried and mixed up, not able to think straight?

7 Food Glorious Food!

Sharing
Eating together gives us the time and the space to talk to one another. We are so busy rushing around or listening to music or watching TV, that it is easy to stop communicating with other people.

Food is important! We all enjoy eating together!

Celebration
Special foods, especially sweet ones, are all a part of throwing a party.

THINGS TO DO

1 Write down a list of all the things that you had to eat yesterday. With the help of your teacher, try to find out how many *calories* were in each item. Then, find out how many calories you need per day to live.

2 Bread is one of the basic foodstuffs. Work in groups of four on the following project about bread. Try to find out:

- how bread is made. Look for some unusual types and if you can, bring some into class to share around
- what *unleavened* bread is, and bring some into the class to try
- what different types of breads there are in the world and how they are made. You may even want to try to make some yourself.

3 Make a class survey of how many times in the week each person sits down with their family for a meal. Also find out how often the family eats out.

4 Think about a meal that you had with family or friends that you really enjoyed. (Think about the people you enjoyed being with, and not just the food!) Talk to the person next to you about this.

5 Design an invitation to a party to celebrate an important personal event (birthday, name day, wedding). Include a menu of the food you will be serving.

Religion and Food

Here is a typical English breakfast being cooked. You can imagine how this smells. This sight and smell would be offensive to people of some religions,(as well as to vegetarians, who do not eat meat). Jews and Muslims do not eat pork (bacon) as it is against the teachings of their religion. There are complicated reasons why some foods are forbidden in some religions.

Food can stand for things in religions, too. Food can be used as a symbol. These pictures show Jewish unleavened bread and Christian hot cross buns. They have special meanings for believers.

Food in Sikhism

During worship in a *gurdwara* , a Sikh place of worship, a sweet paste is handed out to all present, whether they are of the Sikh faith or not. This is called *parshad*. It is a mixture of flour, butter, sugar and water. Eating this together symbolises the fact that we all share one life in one world.

Every gurdwara has a dining room, called a *langar*, and after worship everyone is invited to eat a simple meal - usually a vegetarian curry with chapatis.

Serving food in a Sikh langar.

There was a religious reason for introducing this. Guru Nanak, the founder of the Sikh faith, instructed his followers to eat together to show that they were all equal. The Hindus among whom they lived were divided into *castes*, and higher castes did not sit with the lower castes.

THINGS TO DO

1 Write a short dramatic sketch about a Jewish person coming to a Christian house for breakfast, and finds that bacon and eggs are being cooked. What is the Jewish person's reaction to the sight and smell? How might his or her feelings be explained to the host?

2 Imagine that a group of you are shipwrecked and have been without food for several days. Someone finds an apple and is tempted to eat it all in secret, but then decides against it, says sorry and passes it around for everyone to have a bite. Write a diary entry for that day to say what happened and how you felt about it.

Pesach, the Passover Meal

Pesach (or *Passover*) is a Jewish festival to commemorate the time when the Hebrews were slaves in Egypt. On the night before they left Egypt, led by Moses, they ate a final meal of roasted lamb, bitter herbs, and bread made without yeast, for there was not enough time to allow the bread to rise.

This same food is present on the *Seder plate,* the special symbolic plate placed on the table at the start of the Pesach meal, and is eaten along with an egg roasted in fire, a bowl of salt water and some sweet paste called *charoset,* made from apples, nuts and honey.

A full meal is eaten after this special symbolic food during which the family tell the story of the escape from Egypt, and sing songs. They thank God for his love for them, and ask his blessing for the future.

Jews celebrating Pesach.

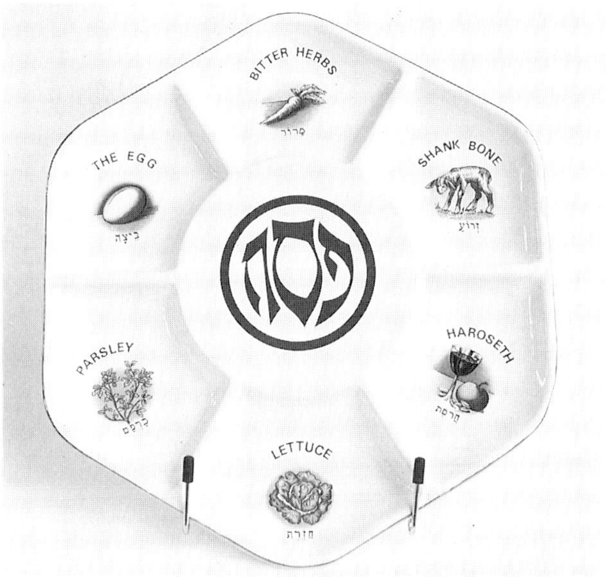

- The lamb and the unleavened bread remind the Jews of the night before the escape from Egypt.
- The bitter herbs remind them of the hard years in Egypt.
- The salt water stands for the tears of the Hebrew slaves
- The roasted egg stands for new life, coming outof suffering.
- The sweet paste stands for freedom and joy.

THINGS TO DO

1 Read the story of the first Passover meal (Exodus 12:1-14 in the Bible).

2 Organise a seder plate in the classroom. All share a piece of unleavened bread and dip this into the salt water and the sweet paste.

3 Draw a diagram of a seder plate. Then write a short sketch in which you meet a Jewish person and ask him or her to explain what all the foods stand for.

Holy Communion

The photographs show Christian services of Holy Communion. The one on the left is a Roman Catholic service, and the other is a Protestant/Free Church service. Different churches have different names for Holy Communion: *Mass, Breaking of Bread, Eucharist, The Lord's Supper*. But it is always bread and wine that is taken and blessed.

Jesus did this himself during his last meal with his disciples. You can read about this in the Gospel of Mark 14:22-25. He took bread and said

"This is my body"

and then he took a cup of wine and said,

"This is my blood."

He told his followers to do this in rememberance of him.

The bread symbolises the body of Jesus, and the wine symbolises his blood. The meal reminds Christians that Jesus died on the cross, and they give thanks that he loved them so much that he was prepared to go through so much suffering.

Christians remember the death of Jesus during the meal. The meal helps them to realise that they share in one faith; they are all in God's family.

Christians believe that Jesus is risen; he is alive, and present in the sharing of bread and wine. This is a mystery, and there are many different ideas of how Jesus is present. All Christians agree, though, that somehow, he is there with them.

THINGS TO DO

1 Draw a cup of wine and a loaf of bread in the middle of a sheet of paper. Around this put three headings, Death, Sharing, Joy. Draw pictures beneath each of the these headings, or stick on pictures cut from magazines and write a sentence for each one saying what Holy Communion symbolises.

8 Trees

Trees can be used as symbols of long life, of life itself, and of mystery.

Long Life

Some trees have been around for hundreds of years. That means that they were planted when your great great-great-great grandparents were alive! Some might even have been alive when Julius Caesar was in Britain over 2000 years ago. Many of these trees are now specially protected. Looking at an ancient tree can make us feel very small - we have been around for such a short time in comparison.

Life

Trees help to support life on earth. Many animals live in their branches, or take shelter beneath them. Trees provide fruit to eat. They also take in carbon dioxide from the air - which is unhealthy for us - and give out oxygen which we can breathe. Sadly, parts of the huge rainforests in tropical areas are being destroyed to build on the land or to grow crops. Many people want to put a stop to this.

Mystery

The photograph on this page shows a dark, gloomy forest. It feels spooky to walk through this - there is little light, there are all kinds of noises and all sorts of shapes of trees. Read this passge from *The Lord of the Rings*. It describes a trip through a dark forest:

> They picked a way among the trees, and their ponies plodded along, carefully avoiding the many writhing and interlacing roots. There was no undergrowth. The ground was rising steadily, and as they went forward it seemed that the trees became taller, darker, and thicker. There was no sound, except an occasional drip of moisture falling through the still leaves. For the moment there was no whispering or movement among the branches; but they all got an uncomfortable feeling that they were being watched with disapproval, deepening to dislike and even enmity. The feeling steadily grew, until they found themselves looking up quickly, or glancing back over their shoulders, as if they expected a sudden blow.

In ancient times, many people thought that forests were sacred places, not only because of the life they supported, but because they were mysterious. Spirits or gods might live there. Even Abraham sometimes went to a forest to pray (look at Genesis 18:1 in the Bible)

THINGS TO DO

1 Write a few paragraphs about being lost in a forest - tell about something you have experienced, or make up a story.

2 Think about the long life of some trees. How would you feel if you looked at a tree that was growing when Caesar was alive?

3 Read Genesis 18 :1-5. Draw a picture of the story, and below it write how you would feel if you were Abraham.

The Tree of Life

The ancient Hebrews told a story to try and explain why there was evil in the world.

When the world began there was a beautiful garden, and a special tree - the Tree of Life - stood in the centre of it. God told the first humans, Adam and Eve, that they could eat any of the fruit in the garden, except the fruit from another tree, the Tree of Knowledge of Good and Evil.

Yet, something disobeyed God in the garden. In the story, evil was there as a serpent. The serpent tempted Adam and Eve, and told them that if they ate from the Tree of Knowledge, then they would be very powerful, like gods. But God had warned them that they would die...

"That's not true: you will not die. God said that because he knows that when you eat it you will become like gods..." replied the serpent.

Eve ate the fruit, and gave some to Adam. They felt different, and hid from God when they heard his voice. God called them to him, and asked what they had done. Adam blamed Eve:

"She made me do it!"

Eve blamed the serpent:

"It made me do it!"

A curse came upon them. They were expelled from the garden, and made to work hard to get food. Gradually, they grew old and died. Suffering and death came into the world. An angel with a flaming sword guarded the garden so none could approach the Tree of Life and live forever.

The story of Adam and Eve in the Garden of Eden is about disobedience, and about being selfish, going your own way and not God's way. If you are selfish it means that you will hurt other people around you. But there is hope at the end of the story. God promised Eve that one of her descendents would break the power of the serpent and lift the curse off the human race.

God said to the serpent:

"Her offspring will crush your head, and you will bite his heel." (Genesis 3:15)

THINGS TO DO

1 Draw a comic strip telling the story of Adam, Eve, and the two trees.

2 Can you think of a time when you disobeyed someone and got into trouble? How quickly did you put things right?

3 Make up a story about someone who gets into trouble with the police, and how he or she is helped afterwards.

The Christian Cross

In their ceremonies and prayers Christians remember the death of their Master on a cross. They sing hymns about it, share bread and wine to remind them of it, and thank God for it in prayers. They even call the day of Jesus' death 'Good Friday'!

Jesus was taken prisoner and nailed to a wooden cross by the Romans. This was a common and cruel way of executing criminals and trouble-makers. You could survive for a couple of days on a cross in excruciating pain. Eventually, your strength would give way, the weight of your body would constrict your lungs until you could not take any more breaths, and you suffocated to death.

Many people suffered for saying things the Romans did not like, and many people still suffer today in some parts of the world where people are not allowed free speech - they might be imprisoned, or beaten, or murdered.

Christians believe that Jesus was not just any man, but God living as a human being. Jesus was fully God and fully human at the same time. They believe that God came to earth, that he suffered at the hands of the Romans, and that he forgave them. He did this although, with his almighty power, he could have saved himself and destroyed them all.

When Jesus died on the cross he said,

'Father, forgive them, for they do not know what they are doing.'

Christians see Jesus as the promised offspring of Eve. He breaks the power of evil and brings blessings. By dying on the cross he has forgiven all sins.

It is as though Jesus has opened the way to the Tree of Life again. Christians see the cross as symbolising the Tree of Life, because it was there that sins were forgiven, so that peace can come to us.

THINGS TO DO

1. Why do you think Christians call the day of Jesus' death 'Good Friday'?
2. Look up these verses in the New Testament and see what they say about the death of Jesus; John 15:12-13, Mark 10:45, Romans 5: 6-11.
3. Draw a large cross, and write on it anything that you would like to see changed in the world, or evils you would want forgiven.

Two More Stories of the Tree of Life

Yggdrasil

The Norse myths (stories of the ancestors of today's Scandinavians) tell of a Tree of Life. This was known as *Yggdrasil*, or the World Ash. All life came from this tree, and its roots supported the cosmos. One root reached Asgard, the world of the gods, one reached Midgard, the world of men and women, and one reached Niflheim, the Underworld. A well stood under the root of the tree leading to Midgard. The dew that fell upon the ground from the tree was like honey. One story tells of the god Odin sacrificing himself to himself upon this tree to find wisdom, and then coming back to life again.

> For nine nights, wounded by my own spear, consecrated to Odin, myself sacrificed to myself, I remained hanging from the tree.

It is not certain how old this story about Odin is, and some think it was based on stories of Jesus dying on the cross.

The Two Trees of Valinor

J.R.R. Tolkien was a modern writer of myths. In his book, *The Silmarillion*, he described the origin of the gods, and the various races who lived on Middle Earth, as a background to his epic story *The Lord of the Rings*. At the beginning of time, he imagines two trees of life:

> And as they watched, upon the mound there came forth two slender shoots; and silence was over all the world in that hour, nor was there any other sound save the chanting of Yavanna. Under her song the saplings grew and became fair and tall, and came to flower; and thus there awoke in the world the Two Trees of Valinor. Of all things which Yavanna made they have the most renown, and about their fate all the tales of the Elder Days are woven. The one had leaves of dark green that beneath were as shining silver, and from each of his countless flowers a dew of silver light was ever falling, and the earth beneath was dappled with the shadows of his fluttering leaves. The other bore leaves of a young green like the new opened beech; their edges were of glittering gold. Flowers wound upon her branches in clusters of yellow flame, formed each to a glowing horn that spilled a golden rain upon the ground; and from the blossom of that tree there came forth warmth and a great light. Each shone for seven hours then grew dim, only to start up again. One would start to shine an hour before the other dimmed.

THINGS TO DO

1. Draw your own version of Yggdrasil and the three worlds.
2. Draw or paint you idea of the Two Trees of Valinor.
3. Write a travel journal entry, pretending that you sit under one of the trees. Say what happened and what you felt.

9 Beginnings

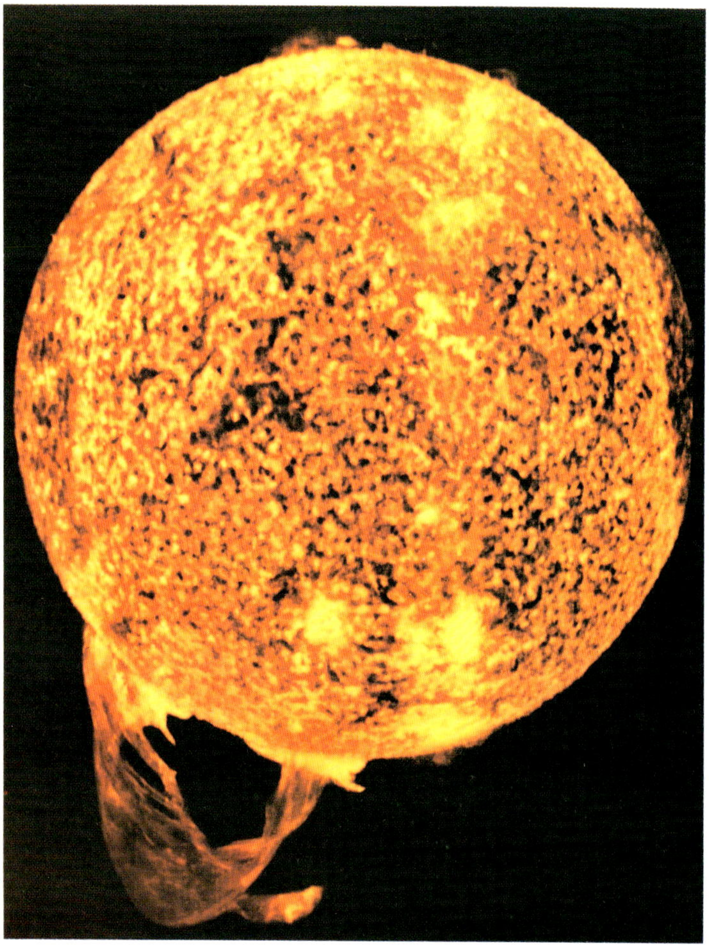

The sun - source of our heat and light - is just one tiny part of a universe that is expanding and cooling.

People are fascinated about how the universe began. They have told stories about this since the dawn of time. Modern scientists tell stories, too. They have many more facts and observations to go on than ancient people. This is one modern story of how the world began:

> There was a tiny, tiny particle of matter, smaller than any human eye can see. This particle was far heavier than the Empire State Building, than the whole world, or the entire universe of galaxies. Nothing else existed. This tiny particle continued to shrink and shrink and shrink, until, one split second, it was all too much! It exploded with a huge bang!
>
> Matter was flung across space. This settled and cooled down. The cooled matter formed the stars and the planets. The galaxies are still expanding outwards into space, rushing away from each other at terrific speeds.
>
> On earth, the third planet from our sun, conditions just happened to be right for the beginning of life. Slowly, over millions of years, life started in the sea, and grew and developed until creatures crawled out onto the land. After years when huge lizards ruled the world, mammals survived and human beings developed from the line of apes. Things slowly evolved to be the way they are now. This development is known as *evolution*.

Yet, complicated as it is, this story only tries to tell us 'how' things came to be. It is not concerned with 'why' all of this should have happened the way it did. Has life occurred by chance, or with a reason? Is there a God, or a Mind behind the universe, guiding it as it has developed?

Ancient people told stories to try to say both 'how' and 'why' there was a world. They believed an intelligence was behind the development of life. Some modern people believe this, while others do not.

THINGS TO DO

1 Draw a comic strip to tell the modern *evolutionary* story of creation.

2 What is the difference between the question 'how' and the question 'why'? For example a freshly baked cake is on the table, waiting for you. The recipe book tells you how it was made, but why did your brother bother to bake it?

3 Do you think that the universe is just here by chance, or that it exists for a purpose?

4 Take a scrapbook and put in it anything you can think of to do with your own origins - the time of your birth - eg photos, birth certificate, write about your parents' memories.

Music and Dancing!

This is a creation story from ancient Mexico.

God made earth, air, water, and all living things. The earth grew jaws like a crocodile, and ate up every living thing it could find. Earth dived into the water and hid there.

Two of the beings that escaped her jaws, Wind and Shadow, decided to attack her and release all the beings she had eaten. They disguised themselves as serpents, and fought with her. Shadow wrapped his coils around her and dragged her to the surface, where parts of her body were torn off. These formed islands and continents.

Wind and Shadow forced her to release all the beings inside her, and then she sank to the bottom of the water again. Occasionally, she still roars and destroys buildings!

Wind and Shadow remade creation, but some of the beings left the world and went to live in the palace of the sun. One day, Wind and Shadow noticed how quiet everything was. The musicians had all gone to live with the Sun. Wind and Shadow journeyed to the Sun's palace and searched for the musicians. They hid from them, and Shadow roared with anger and scared them out into the open. They brought the musicians back to earth, and stood them in the clouds. As they played, flowers opened, trees grew, and beauty filled the world again.

THINGS TO DO

1 What do you think of this story? Is it true in any way?

2 What did the ancient Mexicans mean when they said that the Earth still roared?

3 Beauty returned to the world when the musicians returned. Do you enjoy listening to music? How does this make you feel? Talk about this as a class. Perhaps some music makes you feel excited and full of life, or sad, or very peaceful. Bring some pieces of music into class that make you feel this way and play them.

Choose!

This is a Nigerian story of creation.

Earth knew nothing but savage thunderstorms for a thousand years. Suddenly, the sun broke out and dried the surface of the earth. The mud split apart to make hills and plains.

The Mother of Life, Woyengi, stepped down from heaven in a lightning flash. She gathered handfuls of dust and earth and placed these on the Table of Creation, a huge stone that stood before her. From the dust she made tiny dolls, and then, picking each one up, breathed life into it. The earth figures wriggled and moved about. They had no eyes, and were neither male nor female.

She picked them up again, smoothed open some eyes, and asked them to choose whether to be a man or a woman. She dressed the men in white shirts and the women in white dresses.

The Mother of Life began to speak to the people, and they all fell silent. She had given them life, sight and sex. She asked them to choose what sort of life they wanted.

A babble of voices rose, some asking for riches, some for houses, some for skills of baking or hunting, or building, or of curing the sick. 'So be it,' she said. 'You have chosen'.

She set them down by two rivers. She pointed to one river. 'This leads to luxury and wealth; that one leads to ordinary, humble life,' she told them. They had to choose again. Some stepped into the first stream. It flowed fast and furious and people were frightened. Some wanted to change their minds, but it was too late. The other stream was shallow, cool and clear. Here were the humble, the helpful and the creative people.

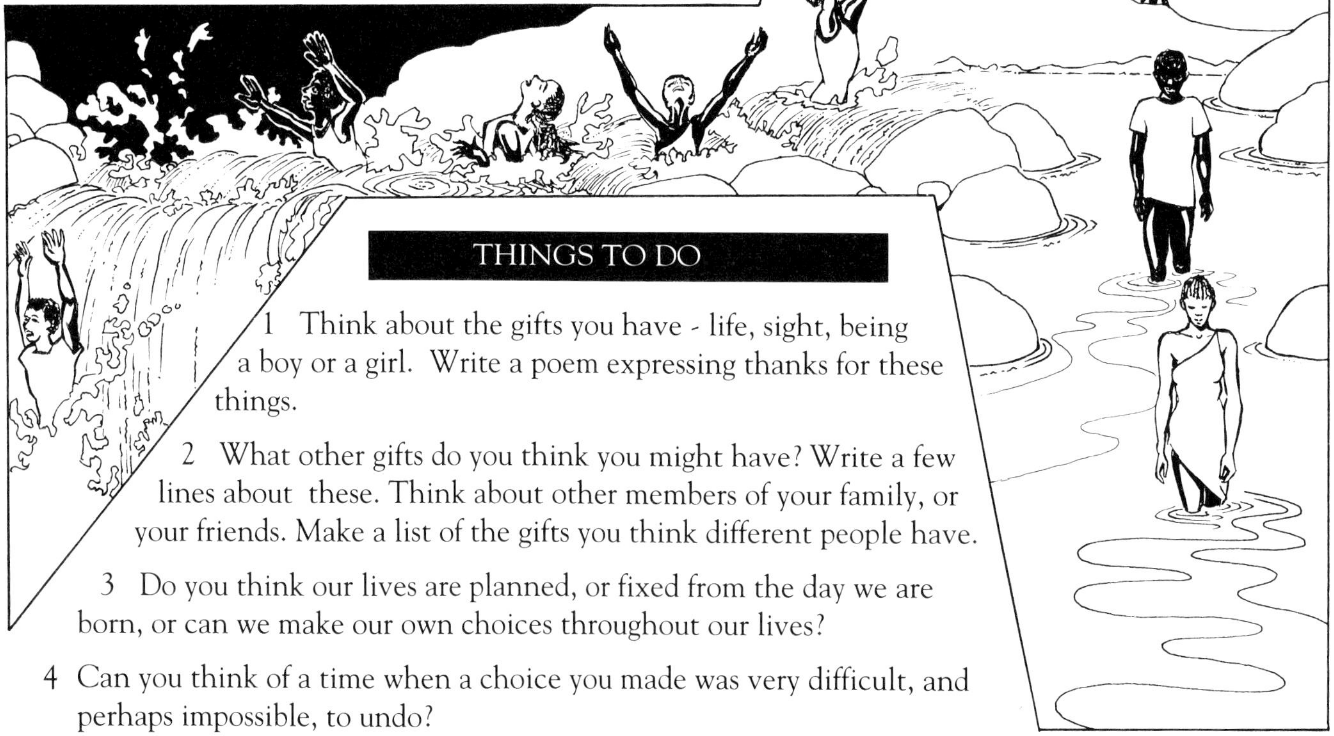

THINGS TO DO

1 Think about the gifts you have - life, sight, being a boy or a girl. Write a poem expressing thanks for these things.

2 What other gifts do you think you might have? Write a few lines about these. Think about other members of your family, or your friends. Make a list of the gifts you think different people have.

3 Do you think our lives are planned, or fixed from the day we are born, or can we make our own choices throughout our lives?

4 Can you think of a time when a choice you made was very difficult, and perhaps impossible, to undo?

5 Why do you think the river that led to wealth was dangerous and fast?

All in a Week's Work!

The ancient Hebrews told a story to describe how God made the world. They imagined this happening in seven days. Each day, God commanded something new to happen.

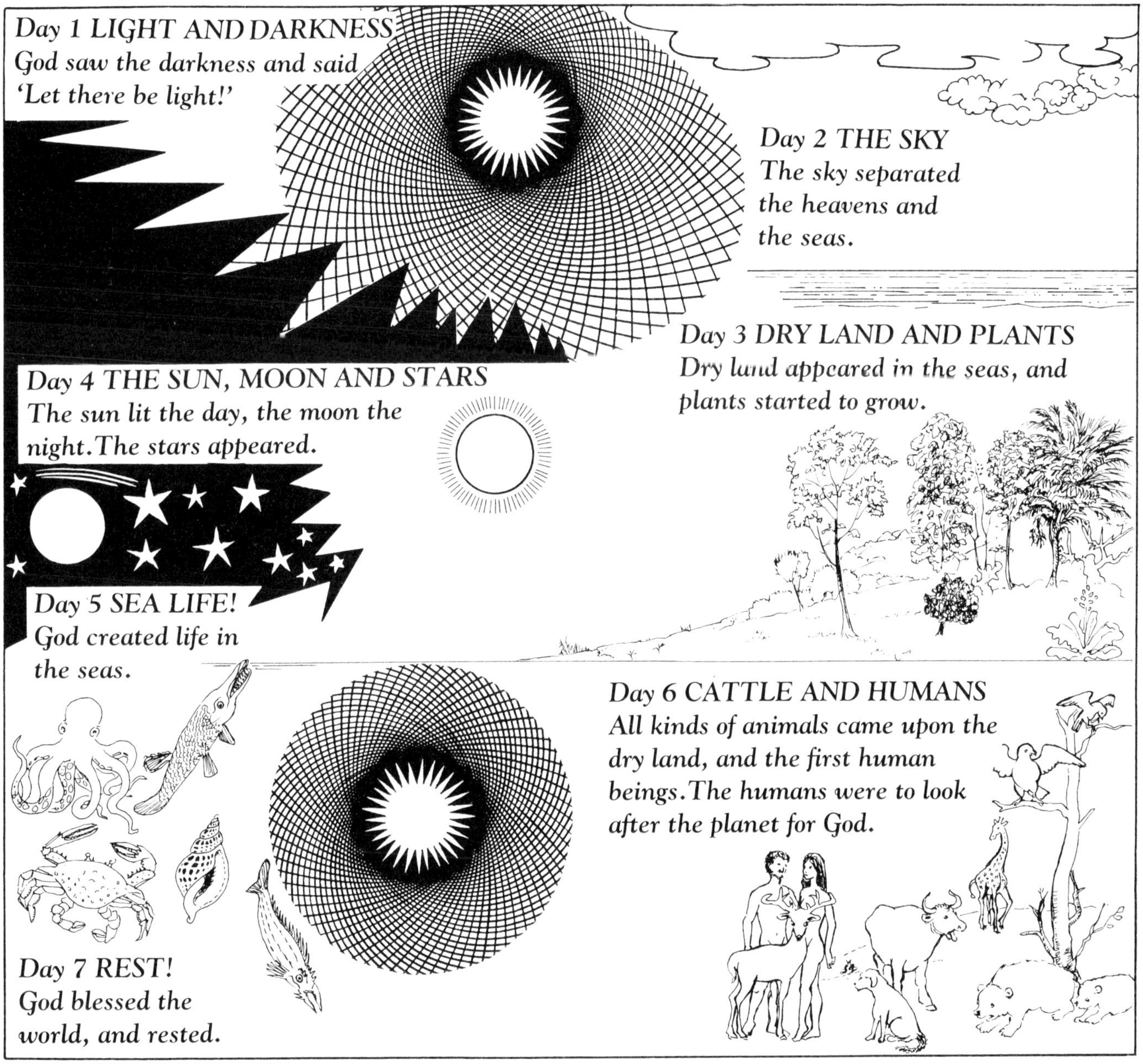

This ancient story can be found in the Bible, Genesis chapter one. The Hebrews were people of faith and did not mean to teach science. They were concerned with 'why' the world was made, not 'how'. Some modern readers take this story as poetry, believing that God made the world over millions of years and not in a week. Some take it word-for-word.

THINGS TO DO

1 Design a large collage as a class, divided into six sections, telling the story of the creation.

2 Read Genesis 1:26-31. What does God expect human beings to do in the world? What were they to eat in the beginning? Why do you think some people choose to be vegetarians today?

10 Endings

People have always wondered how the world will end. They have guessed, and dreamed dreams, and told stories. Everything we know in our life will come to an end. We grow old and die. A tree grows from a seed and eventually dies. Summer turns into autumn, and so on.

It is hard to imagine that the universe could just keep on going.

- Some scientists think that it will, even though many stars and planets will be created and destroyed all the time. Our sun will run out of energy and then our solar system will be no more. But the universe will go on.
- Some scientists think that the universe will come to an end. The galaxies are all expanding, and the universe is getting bigger. One day, it might all collapse in on itself and become very, very small and dense.
- Some think it could burst forth again, in a new 'big bang', and a new universe might be formed. This might be very different from the present one, with different laws of physics.
- This process of death and renewal might just go on happening, with the universe expanding and collapsing forever, or it might happen only once.
- Others think the whole universe will run out of energy and everything will be over - cold, with no life.

Is the universe a place full of stories and adventures like a novel, which comes to an end never to start again? Or does it have a never ending series of sequels? Is the universe just here by chance or does it have a meaning, a purpose? Some think we are here by chance, and some think that God made us and guides us. Believers in God feel that however the universe ends, there must be something more than emptiness.

THINGS TO DO

1 Make a chart showing the various ideas scientists have about what will happen to the universe in the future.

2 How do these different ideas make you feel?

3 Why do you think it difficult for people to imagine something that lasts forever?

4 Write a few paragraphs about what you think you would like to do in your lifetime. You may illustrate this, too.

The Return of Christ

Christians believe that God has a special plan for the universe. One day, Jesus will return, but not as an ordinary person. He will not be born as a baby again, but he will come back as God, in glory. The Gospel of Mark describes this;

> the sun will grow dark, the moon will no longer shine, the stars will fall from heaven, and the powers in space will be driven from their courses. Then the Son of Man will appear, coming in the clouds with great power and glory... (Mark 13:24-26)

The Book of Revelation says this;

> His eyes were like a flame of fire, and he wore many crowns on his head... on his robe, and on his thigh was written the name: 'King of kings and Lord of lords'(Revelation 19:12,16)

Later, the same book says;

> Now God's home is with mankind! He will live with them, and they shall be his people. God himself will be with them, and he will be their God. He will wipe every tear from their eyes. There will be no more death, no more grief or crying or pain. The old things have disappeared. (Revelation 21:3-4)

There are many symbols in these passages from the New Testament - flames, white light, crowns and falling stars. It is difficult to know exactly what they mean.

- Some Christians take all these passages word-for-word. They believe that Jesus will return just as he left. There will be special signs in the sky.
- Others take them as symbols. Perhaps there will be a powerful spiritual awakening all over the world that will change human history. Jesus will return in Spirit.
- Others think the Bible passages are a mixture of facts and symbols. Jesus will return, but no one can really imagine it! It will be a total surprise. Christians believe that the world is here for a purpose, and God has not finished with it yet.

An artist's impression of the Second Coming of Christ

THINGS TO DO

1 Draw or paint a picture based upon one of the passages printed above about the return of Jesus.

2 How do these passages make you feel?

3 Flames, white light, crowns and falling stars - what do you think all these things symbolise? Write a sentence for each one.

Ragnarok

The Vikings told the story of Ragnarok. This was the end of the world of humans and of gods.

There will be a time of wars and fighting all over the world. Then the Monstrous Winter will come. This will be a succession of three, freezing winters, with no summertime in between.

Great wolves are unleashed. One swallows the sun, the other the moon. The stars fall from heaven. The earth and the mountains shake. A great flood bursts upon the world from the depths of the earth, and a huge sea serpent writhes in the ocean. Surtr the fire god rides forth, burning everything in his path. All the gods assemble on the plain of Vigridr.

Battle commences, and Odin is swallowed by one of the wolves. The whole earth is consumed by fire, the World Tree, Yggdrasil, shakes, and the land of the gods crumbles.

The Vikings asked the question; 'But what comes after? What happens when all creation is burned up, when the gods are all dead as well as the chosen warriors and the races of men?

There will be a new earth and a new heaven. Two humans survive, Lif and Lifrasir, along with some of the gods. The god Balder comes back from the world of the dead and joins them. There will be good halls in Okolnir and Nidafjoll, called Brimir and Sindri. There will be peace and an end to war. A Viking poem says of the two humans; 'Lif and Lifrasir themselves will lie hid in Hoddmimir's wood; they shall drink meanwhile of the morning dews and people the plains of Earth.'

THINGS TO DO

1 Create an imaginary diary for the last days of the earth, listing all the events that happen in the story of Ragnarok until Odin's death.

2 Work in groups to create a large painting of the battle of the gods. Have them fight in the world of the gods, and on Earth, with the great Earth Tree down the centre.

Creator, Preserver, Destroyer!

The Hindu religion talks about God as Creator, Preserver and Destroyer. These three aspects of God are represented as three beings - Brahma, Vishnu and Shivah. Brahma creates the galaxies, Vishnu watches over them and Shiva destroys them.

The cycle begins again, when Brahma creates a new world. Creation is a never ending story, going on and on forever. Only God lasts forever.

To help understand what Hindus mean by thinking of God as these three things, think of an artist painting a picture.

She looks at it, touches it up with brush strokes here and there. She covers it up so no one will smudge it or damage it. A little later, she takes it out again and has a good, long look at it. She is unhappy. The painting does not quite say what she wants. She tears it up and takes her brushes to start again.

In the same way, we can think of God as an artist, forever creating and doing new things. Sometimes things have to be destroyed before new things can happen.

THINGS TO DO

1 The idea of God constantly creating and destroying the universe fits in with one modern scientific theory. What is this?

2 How does this idea of the universe make you feel?

3 Think of some examples where something has to end before something new can begin. Talk about this as a class.

4 Write a paragraph about an experience you have had about something ending, but then something new happening.

Teachers' Notes

Chapter 2

Listen, as a class, to the sections of *Joseph and his Amazing Technicolor Dreamcoat* which deal with the relevant parts of the Joseph story.

Read through the first part of *Jonathan Livingstone Seagull* by Richard Bach, where Jonathan learns to fly in new and exciting ways.

Act out the story of Theseus *or*

Split the class into two groups. One group makes a Minotaur mask, and the other makes a Theseus mask. They each, respectively, make a list of all the bad and frightening things in life, and the good, pleasant things. One person should then stand at the front of the class and wear the Minotaur mask. Another should follow suit, wearing the Theseus mask Each should read out their list. At the end have the Minotaur bow down at Theseus' feet, and have the class cheer Theseus.

Chapter 3

Research the full story of Rama and Ravana and present it to the class. It could be made the basis for a dramatic performance or mime.

Read the story of the healing of the blind man in John 9 to the class. Divide the class into groups and have each group act this out in its own way. Perhaps some groups would like to set their performance in modern times.

Organise a 'Festival of Lights' for your class. Everyone should bring a light of some kind, and something to sing, music to listen to, or a short story or poem to read, or a joke to tell. Tbe music and stories should be about things that make people feel happy.

Chapter 4

The following might help pupils appreciate the sense of forgiveness:- Give each pupil a piece of paper. Ask the class to think of things that they have done wrong. Particularly things that have hurt people. Then ask them to write them on their pices of paper. Tell them to fold the paper, to keep what they have written a secret. Collect them in a bin bag, and seal the bag, and explain to the class that it will be taken and destroyed. Following this you could perhaps use a candle flame as a focus of attention. After a few moments reflection, the class might repeat something together, in order to express the hope for a new start. They could say:

"I turn from the past.
I open a door into the future.
I seek peace, I seek joy, I seek friendship".

Chapter 7

Share a fresh loaf of bread around the class. Each person should take a piece and then pass it on.

Invite a local priest or minister to talk to the class about a Holy Communion service, and ask him or her to show them the special cups and plates, and any special robes that he wears.

Chapter 8

You could create a huge Tree of Life picture with the class. It could be painted on wallpaper, stretching this from the classroom floor to the ceiling. Pupils mightg paint a sun rising behind the tree, with rays of light shining out, and then stick on drawings or pictures of animals that would live in a tree or around it.

Trees are important for life on earth, and a good starting point for looking at environmental issues. For those wanting to take practical steps, write for information about tree planting schemes to The Woodland Trust, Autumn Park, Grantham, Lincolnshire NG31 6LL.

Read the account of the Pilgrim losing his burden at the foot of the cross from John Bunyan's *Pilgrim's Progress* to the class.

Chapter9

Pupils could act out the Mexican creation story as a class. Four or five pupils together could take the parts of the Earth, Wind and Shadow.

You could play a variety of musical pieces to the class, and discuss the sort of mood that each evokes.

In looking at the Biblical account of creation, you might arrange a session to perform dances to tell the story of creation. Seven groups of pupils should take one day each. This is also a suitable subject for a wall display, divided into the seven sections.

See also the suggestions for meditations and guided fantasies on pages 6 and 7.